CORNERS of CAMBRIAN

Compiled by Jeffery Grayer

The
· Transport ·
Treasury

Reviving the memories of yesterday…

© Images and design: The Transport Treasury 2024. Text Jeffery Grayer

ISBN 978-1-913251-59-8

First published in 2024 by Transport Treasury Publishing Ltd., 16 Highworth Close, High Wycombe, HP13 7PJ

www.ttpublishing.co.uk

Printed by Short Run Press, Bittern Road, Sowton Industrial Estate, Exeter, EX2 7LW

Front cover: Manor Class No. 7811 *"Dunley Manor"* heads the Aberystwyth portion of the *"Cambrian Coast Express"* (CCE), the premier service on the Cambrian lines, out of Machynlleth on 5th. September 1958. Inaugurated in 1927 the CCE operated Mondays-Fridays during the summer period becoming a Saturday only service with the outbreak of war in 1939. Locomotives were changed at Wolverhampton, to something more suitable for the light track and weight restricted bridges of the Cambrian lines, thus permitting a non-stop run from there to Welshpool via the Abbey Foregate curve at Shrewsbury. The train was reinstated after the war, again Saturday only, but the name was not resurrected until 1951 when daily operations resumed but now running into and out of Shrewsbury where the train reversed. SUM 358

Frontispiece : A member of the footplate crew looks back along his train as Dukedog No. 9004 pauses at Barmouth with a service from Dovey Junction to Pwllheli on 11th. September 1958. SUM 374

Rear Cover : A vintage Cambrian Railways cast iron sign with the previous ownership painted out remains in situ at Dovey Junction along with a more modern "Beware of the Trains" notice on 5th. September 1958. SUM 356

CONTENTS

This glorious panorama epitomises the attraction of the Cambrian Railways system running as it did through some of the most spectacular scenery which the Principality had to offer. In this view, dating from 6th September 1958, a pair of locomotives, comprising a prairie tank and a Dukedog, cross Barmouth Bridge whilst small boats bob gently at their moorings at the mouth of the estuary of the Afon Mawddach. Whilst this structure remains one of the highlights of a trip along the coast today it has also proved to be something of an Achilles heel requiring some expensive restoration work to ensure its survival into the 21st. century. SUM365

INTRODUCTION

As a concise introduction to the gestation of the Cambrian Railways system I can do no better than quote the opening paragraph of a history of the railway written one hundred years ago by one Charles Penrhyn Gasquoine -

"When what eventually became the Cambrian Railways was born it was a very tiny baby. Compared with its ultimate frame, it possessed neither arms nor legs, nor even head, and consisted merely of heart and a small part of its trunk. It began "in the air" at Newtown and ended, if possible, in still more ethereal poise, at Llanidloes. Physical junction with existing lines there was none, and the engines—four in number—which drew the coaches that composed those early trains had to be brought by road, from Oswestry, in specially constructed wagons, not without difficulties and adventures, and placed on the metals at the railhead, to live their life and perform their duty in "splendid isolation." It was only gradually that limb after limb was added, and subsequently constructed railways were incorporated or absorbed, until the consolidated system obtained the rather attenuated proportions with which we are familiar to-day, stretching from Whitchurch, on the Cheshire border, to Aberystwyth, on the shores of Cardigan Bay, with its two chief subsidiary "sections," one (including some half dozen miles of the original track) from Moat Lane Junction to Brecon, and another from Dovey Junction to Pwllheli; shorter branches or connecting lines from Ellesmere to Wrexham, Oswestry to Llangynog, Llanymynech to Llanfyllin, Abermule to Kerry, Cemmes Road to Dinas Mawddwy, Barmouth Junction to Dolgelley, and two lengths of narrow gauge line, from Welshpool to Llanfair Caereinion and Aberystwyth to Devil's Bridge, altogether exactly 300 miles."

As might be expected with the passage of a century since these words were written, much has changed on the former Cambrian Railways system with many line and station closures such that all that remains today of the original 300 miles are the 118 miles of standard gauge from Buttington Junction near Welshpool to Aberystwyth and Pwllheli and the narrow gauge tourist lines of the Welshpool & Llanfair (W&L) and Vale of Rheidol (VoR). Even this remnant of the main line has not been retained without considerable battles against closure and costly repairs over the intervening years. However, preservation has also played a significant part in keeping alive most of the W&L and all of the VoR narrow gauge lines. Standard gauge preservation also has a foothold at Oswestry where Cambrian Heritage Railways operate over a short length of track towards Llynclys where there is also an isolated, for the time being, preservation hub.

In this volume we look back at what was primarily a steam operated railway captured on film by a variety of photographers between the 1930s and 1970s featuring through expresses, locals, branch line services and even the occasional freight not forgetting the infrastructure of stations, sheds, signals and signage. Passing to the Great Western at the Grouping the Cambrian lines became part of the Shrewsbury District of the Western Region of British Railways upon nationalisation with control subsequently passing to the London Midland Region in 1963. Today services are operated by Transport for Wales (TFW).

Contraction of the system had begun back in January 1931 when the Dinas Mawddy branch lost its passenger service the same year that saw the end of services on the Kerry branch although freight lingered on here until 1956. The Tanat Valley line to Llangynog closed in January 1951 and the W&L, which had already closed to passengers in 1931, shut its doors to goods in 1956. The first of the 1960s closures was that of the junction station of Buttington, where the joint line from Shrewsbury joined the Cambrian route, followed by the Ellesmere – Wrexham line which went in September 1962 with closure of the Mid Wales line coming shortly after in

CORNERS of the CAMBRIAN

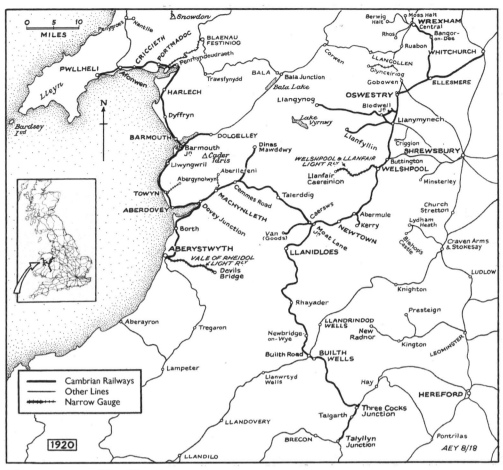

Map courtesy Alan Young.

Shrewsbury and Aberystwyth/ Pwllheli in June 1965. Oswestry still saw trains by way of a shuttle service to Gobowen but this came to an end in November 1966.

In the 21st. Century there remain just four stations open between Shrewsbury and Dovey Junction with a further two between there and Aberystwyth and twenty four on the Pwllheli line of which no fewer than fifteen are request stops. In 2022 there were 12 departures from Aberystwyth and 8 from Pwllheli

December 1962. The former L&NWR link from Caernarvon to Pwllheli via Afon Wen was severed in December 1964 closely followed in January 1965 by closure of the Llanfyllin branch the same date as the Buttington Junction to Whitchurch route closed meaning that services from the rest of the BR network now accessed the Cambrian mainly via the former GWR/LNWR joint line from Shrewsbury. Following flooding on the Ruabon – Barmouth line in December 1965 part of the route never re-opened and a surviving shuttle service from Barmouth to Bala Junction via Dolgellau finished in January 1966. Sections of former double track between Newtown and Moat Lane Junction and between Llanbadarn Crossing and Aberystwyth were singled that year. The line to West Wales from Aberystwyth via Carmarthen closed in December 1964 when floods affected the route near Strata Florida thus severing another link from the Cambrian coast to the wider world. A drastic rationalisation saw the closure of many intermediate stations between

on Mondays-Fridays some of which were through services to Birmingham International although passengers from Pwllheli are required to change at Machynlleth on all services. This volume highlights many of the notable features associated with the Cambrian such as the famous "Dukedog" locomotives which are well represented here as is the line's principal train the "Cambrian Coast Express". Barmouth Bridge and the Friog avalanche shelter are two of the classic subjects beloved by the line's photographers over the years as are examples of the "venerable" motive power captured on film at the line's depots. We also take a look at some of the more remote corners of the Cambrian system such as the rarely photographed branch to Wrexham Central, the former Tanat Valley branch and some of the smaller stations on the Mid Wales route.

Jeffery Grayer,
Devon 2023.

On 30th. May 1961 the up *"Cambrian Coast Express"*, is seen at Dovey Junction with No. 7803 "Barcote Manor" collecting the portion recently arrived from Pwllheli and Barmouth which it will attach to the portion which it has brought in from Aberystwyth. Although the portions of the CCE were joined at Dovey Junction for the up service the split on the down service was more conveniently accomplished at Machynlleth. H2316

Machynlleth based No. 7823 _"Hook Norton Manor"_ waits departure time at Aberystwyth's platform No. 1 on 29th. June 1962 before leaving with the up _"Cambrian Coast Express"_ to Paddington which was due away at 11:45 am. Eight minutes were allowed at Dovey Junction for attaching the portion from Pwllheli. WS6208

Under clear signals No. 7803 *"Barcote Manor"* is about to depart Welshpool, the last stop before reversal at Shrewsbury, with the up CCE on 30th. May 1961. This Manor was one of six based at Machynlleth depot at this date although it was to depart for Croes Newydd shed the following year. H2320

This view, taken from the footbridge at Machynlleth on 31st. May 1961, shows No. 7803 *"Barcote Manor"* with the up CCE. Carriage boards are carried on this occasion and in the distance a pannier tank can be seen undertaking some shunting in the yard. H2365

For the Pwllheli portion of the CCE prairie tanks, such as 4500 Class No. 5541 seen here in this undated view, were often used but nonetheless they still proudly carried an appropriate headboard although this was the plainer version not the one which incorporated a shield with the Cambrian Railways coat of arms consisting of a red English demi-rose on the right and a green Welsh dragon on the left. This more decorative headboard was used from the summer of 1958 until the last titled run of the train on 4th. March 1967. At auction in July 2011 this headboard realised £13,600. REV 281-3

Table 12

CAMBRIAN COAST EXPRESS
RESTAURANT CAR SERVICE (¶)
LONDON, ABERDOVEY, TOWYN, BARMOUTH, PWLLHELI and ABERYSTWYTH

WEEK DAYS

		am			am
London (Paddington)	..dep	10A10	Aberystwyth .. ..dep		11A45
					pm
Banbury General ..	{arr	11 22	Borth .. .. ,,		12A 5
	{dep	11 24	Dovey Junction .. ..arr		12 25
		pm			
Birmingham	{arr	12 13			am
(Snow Hill)	{dep	12 17	Pwllheli .. .. ..dep		9A55
Wolverhampton	{arr	12 39	Criccieth .. .. ,,		10A14
(Low Level)	{dep	12 43	Portmadoc .. .. ,,		10A25
Shrewsbury	{arr	1 19	Harlech .. .. ,,		10A50
	{dep	1 23	Barmouth .. .. .. ,,		11A20
Welshpool	..arr	2 1	Barmouth Junction.. ,,		11A26
Newtown	,,	2 30	Fairbourne .. .. ,,		11A29
Machynlleth	,,	3 20	Llwyngwril .. .. ,,		11A40
			Tonfanau .. .. .. ,,		11 48
Machynlleth ..	..dep	3 40	Towyn .. .. .. ,,		11A59
Penhelig Halt ..	..arr	4 2			pm
Aberdovey	,,	4 6	Aberdovey .. .. .. ,,		12A 6
Towyn	,,	4 14	Penhelig Halt .. .. ,,		12 10
Tonfanau	,,	4 21	Dovey Junction ..arr		12 23
Llwyngwril	,,	4 32			
Fairbourne	,,	4 40	Dovey Junction .. ..dep		12A33
Barmouth Junction ..	,,	4 44	Machynlleth .. .. ,,		12A43
Barmouth	,,	4 50	Newtown .. .. .. ,,		1 35
Harlech	,,	5 17	Welshpool .. .. .. ,,		2 7
Portmadoc..	,,	5 38	Shrewsbury	{arr	2 42
Criccieth	,,	5 50		{dep	2 52
Pwllheli	,,	6 10	Wolverhampton	{arr	3 31
			(Low Level)	{dep	3 35
Machynlleth	..dep	3 25	Birmingham	{arr	3 55
Borth	..arr	3 45	(Snow Hill)	{dep	4 0
Aberystwyth	,,	4 5	Leamington Spa	{arr	4 23
			General	{dep	4 25
			London (Paddington) ..arr		6 0

A—Seats can be reserved in advance on payment of a fee of 2s. 0d. per seat (see page 23).

¶—Restaurant Car available between London (Paddington) and Aberystwyth, in each direction.

Headboard and 1958 timetable for the Cambrian Coast Express

Above. Dukedog No. 9013, rostered to the Pwllheli portion of the CCE together with an unidentified prairie tank, is seen here at Machynlleth on 5th. September 1958 after departure of the portion for Aberystwyth. Some 20 minutes were allowed for the splitting of the train here and the despatch of the Aberystwyth carriages together with its restaurant car before this portion of the train was scheduled to leave. On the far left can be seen the former premises of the Corris Railway terminus. SUM 359

Below. Sporting the new headboard introduced that summer No. 4549 leaves Barmouth with the five coaches comprising the portion of the up CCE from Pwllheli on 11th. September 1958. This would be combined with the Aberystwyth portion at Dovey Junction and ten minutes after arrival of the Pwllheli portion the combined train would depart for its next stop at Machynlleth. This service was one of the few named trains where the headboard was regularly sported by a tank locomotive. SUM 375

Above. Dukedogs were synonymous with the Cambrian lines and here No.9013 is seen in 1952 outside Aberystwyth shed. Given the number 3213, it was constructed in July 1937 from the frames of No. 3374 and the boiler of No. 3257. Although the name *"Earl of Powis"* was allocated this was never carried. It was a long time resident of Aberystwyth shed but its final allocation was Machynlleth from where it was withdrawn in December 1958. NS 200148A

Right.In this undated view No. 9000 is seen at Pwllheli taking water from the platform end water crane. It was initially given the name *"Earl of Mount Edgcumbe"* although this was removed in June 1937 only a year after construction in May 1936. Initially given the number 3200 it utilised the frames of No. 3422 and the boiler of No. 3288. Like many of the class it ended its days, now numbered 9000, allocated to Machynlleth being withdrawn from there in March 1955. NS 201151

No. 9005 running light engine trundles across Barmouth Bridge whilst pedestrians and cyclists make use of the adjacent footway. It carries a shedplate 89A which indicates its home depot was Oswestry from where it would be withdrawn in July 1959. A small charge was made for crossing the bridge by foot or by bicycle and this continued until 2013 after which time payment of tolls became voluntary. It now forms part of National Cycle route No. 8 from Cardiff to Holyhead. Following an examination of the structure in 1980 it was discovered that a species of naval shipworm had wreaked havoc on half of the timber section but fortunately six years later this had been treated and the bridge re-opened. REV 284-3

Dukedog No. 9026 seen in the glorious countryside near Newtown at an unrecorded date in 1950 epitomises the delights of the scenic Cambrian lines.
NS201210

Above. Sacking over a locomotive chimney often indicated that it was stored for the winter awaiting the arrival of an increase in traffic the following summer but in the case of No. 9020, seen here at Oswestry on 30th. June 1956, reinstatement would never come. Following the end of the 1955 summer timetable this Dukedog was put in to store but its services were not required for the 1956 season and it remained in store until withdrawal came in July 1957. AEB B1429

Top right. With steam to spare No. 9012 rolls in to Towyn on 25th. July 1951 with a service for Pwllheli. Castle Class No. 5055, previously named *"Lydford Castle"*, received the name *"Earl of Eldon"* in 1937 from No. 9012 when it was felt that the landed gentry should be commemorated by rather more prestigious locomotives than the distinctly "old fashioned" looking Dukedogs. RCR 3267

Bottom right. On 30th. September 1960, just a month before withdrawal of the last examples, No. 9017, one of the last pair in service at this date together with No. 9014, is seen at Llwyngwril situated between Towyn and Fairbourne with a service to Pwllheli. Constructed in March 1938 and numbered 3217 it had utilised the frame of No. 3425 and the boiler of No. 3258. The passing loop seen here has now been removed and the station is one of the many unstaffed halts on the Cambrian Coast line but still recorded a respectable 19,468 passengers using it in 2021/2. 15440

Above. No. 3287 *"Mercury"* with its crew proudly posing for the photographer is seen here on Aberystwyth shed on 3rd. June 1946. This "Duke" class 4-4-0 started life in 1899 as No. 3321 but was renumbered 3287 in 1912. It was further renumbered some five months after this image was taken becoming No. 9087 in November 1946. The fitting of a 3,500 gallon tender in 1930 created a draught problem as the tender was wider than the cab. This problem was overcome by the fitting of cab sheets to some members of the Duke class that had these wider tenders to improve the air flow however No. 3287 was not so fitted. It was not one of the class that donated its boiler to become part of a "Dukedog" and was to become an early casualty being withdrawn in July 1949. Note the unusually high placement of the cabside number. RCR 1237

Top left. On 30th. April 1960 No. 9014 was used in tandem with Manor Class No. 7827 *"Lydham Manor"* to operate a portion of the annual Festiniog Railway Society special which is seen here at Minffordd where passengers joined the narrow gauge line. The special had originated from Paddington with County Class No. 1021 *"County of Montgomery"* hauling the train to Ruabon where the Manor and Dukedog had taken over for the run through Corwen and Barmouth to Minffordd. The previous year two Dukedogs, Nos. 9018 and 9004, had operated the leg from Ruabon but 1960 was to prove to be the final year when these 4-4-0s played a part in these specials as the final pair was withdrawn in October 1960. HORNE 4485

Bottom left. Dukedog No. 3216, allotted the name *"Earl St. Aldwyn"* which was never carried, is seen at Welshpool station on 7th. June 1946. This locomotive was a 1937 amalgamation of the boiler of No. 3282 and the frames of No. 3404 and would be renumbered 9016 in August 1946 lasting in service until July 1957. RCR1257

WHITCHURCH - OSWESTRY - WELSHPOOL

Above. With the station clock coming up to 4pm a DMU arrives at Whitchurch with a Crewe to Shrewsbury service providing a connection for the Oswestry train standing in the bay platform headed by Standard tank No. 80080. Whitchurch, situated on the main LNWR route from Shrewsbury to Crewe, was where the Cambrian Railways (CR) mainline began. Behind the Standard tank lies the goods yard and stabling point where the former sub shed was located. Whitchurch had also been the junction for services to Chester but this route closed to passengers in 1957 although it was used as a diversionary route for some trains until December 1963. NF 20607

Top left. This footplate view was taken from the cab of No. 9017 at Barmouth Junction on 30th. September 1960 shortly before withdrawal of this, one of the last pair of Dukedogs in operation, the following month. Fortunately this locomotive was the subject of a preservation appeal and thanks to the good offices of the District Locomotive Superintendent at Oswestry was placed in store throughout 1961 to allow time for funds to be raised. It now resides on the Bluebell Railway in Sussex a long way from its former North Wales home. In preservation it has been given the name *"Earl of Berkeley"* a name it was originally allotted but never carried. It has not steamed since 2011 and is currently awaiting overhaul. 15444

Bottom left. Running light engine No. 9016 has just left the Friog avalanche shelter en route to Barmouth on 28th. July 1951. The crew on the footplate are no doubt marvelling at the precarious position from which the photographer has obtained his shot perched as he must have been on the vertiginous cliffs hereabouts. No. 9016 would be withdrawn from Machynlleth shed in July 1957. RCR 3297

Above. With sunlight bringing out the details of the motion No. 9027 is seen on Whitchurch shed on an unrecorded date in 1956. This was an Oswestry based locomotive and would shortly go into store there to await its fate which the following year resulted in withdrawal in August 1957 after a working life of just over 18 years as a hybrid "Dukedog" locomotive during which time it had clocked up a total mileage of 395,007. GE 235

Top left. Just beyond the signalbox, named "Whitchurch Cambrian Junction" at the south end of the station, the CR line can be seen diverging to the right. Weekday departures for CR line stations during the last full winter timetable, 1963/4, were by no means frequent being at 03:15, 07:55, 09:45, 13:30, 16:30, 18:15 (Except Saturdays and School Holidays) and 18:50. Sundays saw just one train leave for Ellesmere and Oswestry but at the rather ungodly hour of 03:15. NF 206-05

Bottom left. Almost new Ivatt 2-6-0s Nos. 46458 and classmate 46457 are seen on Whitchurch shed on 9th. July 1950. This was a 4 road sub shed of Crewe South (5A) and remained open until 1957 although locomotives continued to visit for some time afterwards. Both locomotives were constructed in May 1950 and initially allocated to Crewe North before being transferred to Workington later that year. HG 0598

This view looking east shows the driver of Collett 0-6-0 No. 2237 collecting the token under the watchful eye of the signalbox on the approach to Ellesmere with a service from Whitchurch to Oswestry on 20th. September 1958. An extensive goods yard and sidings and Goods Shed were provided here together with a loading bank for livestock and a 2 ton crane. An unidentified pannier tank can be seen shunting the yard. 4226

A westbound service for Welshpool arriving at Ellesmere powered by Manor Class No. 7802 *"Bradley Manor"* passes the ornate platform canopy provided for the main station building. A few passengers are awaiting the train's arrival including a mother with a pram who will no doubt find travelling by public transport much less convenient once the rail service has been withdrawn. In 1963/4 Ellesmere saw 2 departures for Aberystwyth, 3 for Oswestry and 3 for Welshpool on weekdays with just one departure for Oswestry on Sundays. No. 7802 is one of nine members of the class preserved and is currently based on the Severn Valley Railway. HPW 013

This external view of Ellesmere station shows the imposing nature of the building provided here. Originally part of the Oswestry, Ellesmere and Whitchurch Railway it was opened in May 1863 as a terminus of the line from Whitchurch. The section on to Oswestry did not open until July 1864 when various companies amalgamated to form Cambrian Railways. Following closure to passengers in January 1965 Ellesmere continued to handle goods traffic until the end of March that year. The main building survived as office accommodation for many years and has been given a Grade II listing. Recently planning permission has been given to convert the main building into flats and to develop the remainder of the extensive railway site for housing. HW 265

Above. The interior of Oswestry shed reveals the unmistakeable shape of a Dukedog in the form of No. 9001 seen here on 21st. July 1951. The shed located here and coded variously 89A, 89D and then 6E following the Midland Region takeover from September 1963 was a four road dead end shed with a two road open ended shed attached being the largest depot on the Cambrian system. It retained an allocation of about 30 locomotives with an attendant complement of 100 staff even into its final years before closure came in 1965. RCR3217

Top left. This informative running in board at Ellesmere listed the main stations on the branch to Wrexham but not the numerous halts which were opened later in a bid to boost traffic. By the time of closure there were no fewer than nine intermediate stops on this 12¾ mile branch. Originally conceived as part of a through route to by-pass the dominant GWR lines in the area this destiny was never fulfilled with the line remaining simply a rural branch. At the time of construction of the line Wrexham was the largest town served by the Cambrian Railways. MP 90299

Bottom left. No. 1428 has just arrived at Oswestry on 21st. July 1951 with the shuttle service from the main line at Gobowen. This was to prove the last rail connection to serve Oswestry until it too was withdrawn in November 1966. No. 1428 was to finish its service at Gloucester's Horton Road shed in June 1959. An advertisement of interest on the down platform is that for Stephens' Ink invented in 1832 by one Dr Henry Stephens. His indelible "blue-black writing fluid" was to become famous as Stephens' Ink forming the foundation of a successful worldwide company for over 130 years. RCR 3223

Above. Also seen at Oswestry after arrival on 30th. May 1961 with a service from Llanfyllin is No. 46519. There were only four departures on Mondays – Fridays from the branch terminus to the junction at Llanymynech with an additional service on Saturdays most of which worked through to Oswestry. So with such a limited service it perhaps came as no surprise that the line was included for withdrawal in the Beeching Report. H2336

Top left. The branch train from Llanfyllin has just arrived at Oswestry's up platform headed by one of Ivatt's 2MT 2-6-0s, No. 46516, the usual motive power provided for this service in latter days. This locomotive was allocated to Oswestry from new in 1953 although later that year it was re-allocated to Brecon until it returned to Oswestry in October 1959 remaining at 89C until transfer to Speke Junction in January 1965. HORNE 4584

Bottom Left. The Gobowen shuttle service waits in the bay platform at Oswestry on 30th. May 1961 headed by 6400 Class 0-6-0PT No. 6419. These locomotives introduced by Collett in 1932 were a variation of the 5400 Class with smaller wheels and were pull-push fitted. The former GWR station is seen in the background to this view and after GWR trains were diverted into the Cambrian station the former GWR station was used for goods traffic until 1971 being later demolished with a road being built through the site. In its final years a single car DMU operated the Gobowen shuttle with more than twenty journeys being provided daily over this 2½ mile route in 1963/4 for example. H 2337

Above. Taken from a service from the Llanfyllin branch to Oswestry this is the approach to Pant station which had the suffix (Salop) appended in 1924 to distinguish it from similarly named stations near Wrexham and in Glamorganshire. An older form of transport in the form of the weed choked Montgomery Canal, officially abandoned in 1944, can be seen on the right. In recent years much restoration work has been done on this canal and half its length is now "in water" with current plans to restore it in the vicinity of Pant. HORNE 4583

Top left. Duke Class No. 9084 runs into Llynclys with a mixed down freight including several cattle wagons on 6th. April 1951. Dating from 1899 this veteran was one of only ten of the class to pass into BR ownership but would last in service for only another month after this image was taken being withdrawn in May 1951 from Oswestry shed. Initially carrying the name *"Jersey"*, it was renamed *"Isle of Jersey"* in 1904 the revised nameplate being evident in this image. NS201211

Bottom left. Standard tank No. 80098 is certainly more modern motive power as it comes to a halt at the attractive station of Llynclys in this early 1960s view. In 1964, the year before closure, Llynclys enjoyed 10 up and 11 down services Mondays to Fridays with an extra two down services on Saturdays. There was just one train each way on a Sunday. Apart from a solitary railway employee the platform appears devoid of passengers on this occasion as was so often the case during the later years. NF 206-33

Manor Class No. 7813 *"Freshford Manor"* is about to depart from Llanymynech on 30th. May 1961 with a service for Oswestry. Although many of the class worked on Cambrian lines over the years this example was never allocated to any depot in the area and indeed at this time it was some way from home being based at Tyseley near Birmingham carrying the appropriate 84E shedplate. H2324

The running in board at Llanymynech, seen here on 30th. May 1961, proclaimed this as the junction for the branch to Llanfyllin. Lake Vyrnwy also gets a mention although passengers wishing to travel here would be faced with a 10 mile road journey from the rail terminus at Llanfyllin. The lake is actually a reservoir constructed in the 1880s by flooding the head of the Vrynwy valley and submerging the village of Llanwddyn in order to provide water for Liverpool. Underneath the board a rake of mineral wagons can be seen parked on the grass grown tracks of the old Shropshire & Montgomery railway line. H2326

Llanymynech was at one time the junction for the ill fated Potteries, Shrewsbury & North Wales Railway later resurrected as the Shropshire & Montgomeryshire Railway whose curving platform is seen here in this view also taken on 30th. May 1961. The S&MR closed to passengers in 1933 but it continued to run goods and mineral trains until it was taken over by the War Department in 1941. Returned to civilian status in 1947 it was later nationalised with the Western Region and the War Department sharing ownership. WD usage continuing until 1959 and indeed a WD sign prohibiting entry can be seen at the end of the platform here. March 1960 was to see the last special run from Shrewsbury to Llanymynech over the S&M with formal closure following although the goods yard at Shrewsbury Abbey terminus continued in use as an oil depot until 1988. H2325

Left. Having exchanged tokens No. 7802 *"Bradley Manor"* gets away from Pool Quay negotiating the level crossing over the A438 at the head of the SLS "Farewell to the Cambrian Railways" special of 17th. January 1965. This train was originally scheduled to run on 22nd. November 1964 to mark the closure of the line between Welshpool (Buttington Junction) and Whitchurch but the closure was postponed until 18th. January 1965. The Manor operated the special from Shrewsbury to Welshpool thence via Llanymynech to Oswestry where No. 46512 took tour participants for a trip down the Llanfyllin branch after which they returned to Oswestry and proceeded to Ruabon whence the Manor returned the special to Shrewsbury. A signal box containing 20 levers and dating from provision of the passing loop in 1896 controlled this busy level crossing. NF 207/12

Top left. On the occasion of the Stephenson Locomotive Society (Midland Branch) tour of 21st. September 1958 0-6-0ST No. WD 188 is at the head of the return leg to Shrewsbury Abbey station. The stock consisted of a brake van and three coaches and is seen here awaiting the "right away" in the S&M branch platform at Llanymynech. The tour had begun earlier in the day at Shrewsbury Abbey with the train proceeding to Kinnersley Junction where two return trips by Drewry railcar down the branch to Criggion were made before WD188 continued on to Llanymynech. WD188, formerly WD 75294, a Hunslet 0-6-0ST built by the Vulcan Foundry in 1945 was transferred to the S&MR until closure of that line on 31st. March 1960. Moving to the main WD workshops at Bicester until September 1962 it was subsequently moved to Shoeburyness before being scrapped by Cashmore's at some date after August 1967. AEB 4262

Bottom left. Opened by the Oswestry & Newtown Railway in May 1860 a passing loop at Pool Quay station was not added until 36 years later when a second wooden platform was provided. This was replaced by a concrete structure at sometime during the 1950s. The station's name is said to derive from the fact that it lay at the upper limit of navigation for commercial vessels on the River Severn. A single siding was provided for goods traffic with the yard closing in May 1964. NF 207/11

Top left. By the spring of 1966 track recovery on closed sections of the Cambrian line was proceeding apace with the section between Buttington junction and Pool Quay amongst the first to go. The section from Whitchurch to Ellesmere was left in place for the time being although that from Ellesmere onwards towards Oswestry was also in the process of being lifted. This post closure view of Pool Quay reveals that track was still in position embedded in the tarmac of the A438 and that the crossing gates remain in situ. Beyond all is desolation with the station succumbing to demolition in 1978 to allow the main road to be realigned through the station site and along part of the former trackbed. NF 251-15

Bottom left. The first of three views of Buttington Junction shows Manor Class No. 7811 *"Dunley Manor"* passing through on 3rd. August 1955 with the down *"Cambrian Coast Express"* service working over the former joint GWR/LNWR route from Shrewsbury. Buttington was the junction of the Cambrian line from Whitchurch and the joint line with the latter going on to eclipse the former, becoming the preferred route for through services into mid Wales, leading to the ultimate closure of the Cambrian route from Whitchurch through Oswestry. LRF 1590

Below. On the same date in 1955 the photographer also captured a service from Oswestry to Welshpool which has just departed from Buttington Junction with No. 46515 at the head of its two coach train. A small goods yard lay to the right with further sidings apparent on the left of this view. Upon opening in 1860 the station here was named Cefn but only a month later was renamed Buttington and upon the opening of the line from Shrewsbury two years later became a junction being substantially rebuilt with additional platforms in 1893. The goods yard here closed along with the station in September 1960. LRF 1591

Above. This post closure view of the remains of Buttington Junction taken from an up service to Shrewsbury reveals that the former Cambrian line to Oswestry on the left has been singled. In 1964 the double track between Buttington and Welshpool reverted to its pre-1893 arrangement of two bi-directional single tracks with the former up line becoming the Oswestry line and the former down line becoming the Shrewsbury line. The junction was removed at Buttington and the signal box closed. This situation did not obtain for long however for in January 1965 the Oswestry line closed and track lifting began later that year leaving just a single track to Shrewsbury passing through the former station which by the 1970s had been demolished leaving no trace. LRF 60958

Top right. Welshpool was one of the most important intermediate stations on the route and this was reflected in its magnificent station building constructed in a French renaissance style. The large running in board seen on the up platform proclaimed that it was the "Junction for Shrewsbury, Stafford, Birmingham and London" although of course the physical junction was at Buttington. At the down platform is Manor Class No. 7807 "Compton Manor" whilst 4300 Class No. 7330 can be seen on the right. Although this image is undated the 2-6-0 was withdrawn from Shrewsbury shed in September 1962. HORNE 4540

Bottom right. The up *"Cambrian Coast Express"* is signalled away from Welshpool with No. 7818 "Granville Manor" displaying the appropriate headboard. This 4-6-0 dating from 1939 was withdrawn in January 1965 and scrapped at Cashmore's Great Bridge yard in April that year. Welshpool now has to make do with a much rationalised single island platform opened on a slightly different alignment in 1992 whilst a road now follows the original trackbed and the original Grade II listed station building has a new lease of life as a shop and cafe. HORNE 4565

Standing in the up bay platform No. 4 with two coaches forming the 12:15pm service on 30th. May 1961 is No. 7813 *"Freshford Manor"*. This provided a connection from the up *"Cambrian Coast Express"*, which had departed Welshpool seven minutes earlier, for stations to Oswestry and after a protracted wait there for stations onwards to Whitchurch. H2322

WELSHPOOL – DOVEY JUNCTION – ABERYSTWYTH

This view from 1956 shows the attractive Forden station looking up the line towards Welshpool, the line from here to there having been doubled in 1925. The signalbox, a Dutton type 3, survived withdrawal of passenger services in 1965 but closed in 1969 when reversion to single track occurred. However, it remains in situ today. Typical of so many country stations white washed stones border the platform shrub and flower beds whilst the milepost records a distance of 38¼ miles from the Cambrian line junction at Whitchurch.

Forden sees the arrival of the now preserved No.2516 entering the station from the west with a freight service. The signalman can be seen descending the steps of his box ready to receive the single line token from Montgomery from the crew of the Dean Goods. No. 2516 which was withdrawn in 1956 spent many years inside the old Swindon Museum which opened in 1962 before moving to the new "Steam" museum which opened in 2000 in part of the former GWR Works site at Swindon. AHL

Above. No. 7818 *"Granville Manor"*, with white painted embellishments to the smokebox door handle and the buffers, passes the stone built goods shed at Newtown prior to entering the station with an up service on 31st. May 1961. A down service waits at the opposite platform for the Manor to clear the single line onwards to Moat Lane Junction. H2362

Top left. Abermule, forever associated with the accident which occurred near here on 26th. January 1921 involving a head on collision between trains in which seventeen people were killed, sees the departure of No. 3270 *"Earl of Devon"* as it negotiates the level crossing at the north east end of the station with an up service. Although the date of the image is unrecorded it was probably sometime in the 1930s as the locomotive was withdrawn from service in April 1939. The station house seen on the far right is still in situ today next to the now automated crossing over the remaining single track. GW 253

Bottom left. This view of Abermule station taken from a down train on 31st. May 1961 shows the disused branch platform formerly served by trains to Kerry. Passenger services were withdrawn on this branch back in 1931 but goods traffic had lingered on until 1956. Five years on buffer stops mark the end of branch metals although there still appears to be some freight traffic handled in the small goods yard on the right. Abermule station would still have another five years of life not closing until 14th. June 1965. H 2361

Above. An unidentified Class 37 waits at Newtown with a short train of Presflo wagons whilst a DMU approaches from the west. In addition to the Presflo traffic there is obviously still some wagon load freight being handled in the small goods shed on the right. Some attention is being given to possibly a loose rail chair by two gangers on the up line. The signalbox seen in the distance was originally known as Newtown South until closure of the North box in 1920. The bay platform on the far left had originally been used for branch services to Llanidloes but this soon changed to allow them to begin and end their journeys at Moat Lane Junction. NF 250-33

Top right. This 1952 scene at Moat Lane Junction shows Jones Goods, formerly Cambrian Railways No. 15 later GWR No. 844, shunting wagons in the yard with the main station building in the background. The class dated from 1903 and sixteen were produced known as Class 15 being the final 0-6-0 design built for Cambrian Railways and the first Cambrian locomotives to have Belpaire fireboxes. They were rebuilt by the GWR in the 1920s/30s with new boilers with all, except a solitary example, being given the Standard No. 9 superheated boiler. Under the GWR they were known as class 89. When the Mid Wales line was upgraded to yellow route status in 1940 these locomotives were allowed to operate along it although at restricted speed. The last trio of these 0-6-0s was withdrawn in October 1954 with No. 844 going in August of that year having completed its railway service as a stationary boiler at Oswestry Works. NS 200132B

Bottom right. 1952 is also the year of this view of a train standing at the Mid Wales platform at Moat Lane Junction with Dean Goods No. 2327 at its head. Dating from 1884 time was nearly up for this veteran as it would be withdrawn from Oswestry shed in April the following year just shy of 70 years of service. NS200576B

Above. With part of the station visible in the left background Dean Goods No. 2556 still wearing the early British Railways lettering on its tender is positioned on the turntable at Moat Lane Junction on 14th. July 1952. Carrying an 89A Oswestry shedplate this locomotive, dating from 1897, would be transferred to its final shed Hereford in February the following year from where it would be withdrawn in June 1953. Three years after this view was taken the original locomotive shed here was destroyed in a gale in 1955 being replaced in 1957 with a new corrugated structure. NS200576C

Right. No. 7801 *"Anthony Manor"* runs in to the up platform at Moat Lane Junction from the west with a service for Shrewsbury on an unrecorded date in 1960. Although outnumbered by railway staff there are a few passengers waiting who may well have travelled up the Mid Wales line to this remote junction as there was little habitation in the vicinity to attract local clientele. The nearest settlement of any size was Caersws a mile or so away but this had its own station. The Refreshment Room on the down platform, which was not operated by BR, does not look particularly open whilst in the left background an Ivatt 2-6-0, which had probably brought in the Mid Wales service, can be seen on the depot which was situated between the Cambrian main and Mid Wales lines. Nothing now remains of this former junction station apart from a small section of one of the platforms. NS201202B

Taken from the footbridge at the eastern end of Moat Lane Junction this shot reveals an unidentified BR Standard Class 4 taking water from the platform mounted water crane. Several photographers are seen by the boarded crossing and by the water tower taking the opportunity afforded by the protracted stop here to capture the scene on film. Whilst the fireman attends to the water bag the driver takes the opportunity to inspect the motion of his mount. The signalbox here, one of two provided at the junction was designated "East" and was a product of Dutton & Co. of Worcester. Opening in 1890 it contained a 45 lever frame and the building is slightly non-standard in appearance as the roof line is lower at the rear to accommodate a small extension. The rural nature of the attractive scenery hereabouts is very apparent with a herd of cows grazing in a field adjoining the railway. AEB 1418

Although Caersws station was threatened with closure following the publication of the Beeching Report, along with many other stations on the former Cambrian main line, it was reprieved by the Minister of Transport in December 1964 due to its perceived ability to act as a railhead for nearby Llanidloes which of course had lost its own station when the Mid Wales line closed in 1962. It remains open today with some 22 miles separating it from the next station at Machynlleth, reputedly the longest distance between stations in the whole of Wales. It was once the junction for the Van Railway opened in 1871 and closed in 1940 which was promoted to carry lead from the mines at Van to the Cambrian mainline. MC10011C

Not being as fortunate as Caersws, Carno station is seen in 1962 some 3 years before its closure as part of the Beeching proposals. The village of Carno was probably best known as the home of the Laura Ashley textile company which was based here from the 1960s until its closure in 2005. The site, which incorporates the old station, was sold to West Yorkshire Fellmongers the UK's largest suppliers of sheepskin and lambskin. For the past 20 years or so there has been a vigorous local campaign to re-open the station which has the backing of the Welsh Government. NS 201146

Above. For locomotive crews tackling the severe 1 in 52 grade through a 120 foot deep cutting in solid rock up to Talerddig summit at 693 feet above sea level, sight of the signalbox, seen here in 1977, was no doubt a welcome relief. The box, originally to a McKenzie & Holland type 1 design and built for Cambrian Railways in the 1870s contained an 18-lever frame though this was later replaced by a frame made by Dutton & Co. In the late 1960s a GWR Vertical Tappet frame of 18 levers was installed even though the line fell, by this date, within the London Midland Region. It closed in 1988 when the RETB (Radio Electric Token Block) system, which was controlled from Machynlleth thus rendering all other signalboxes on the line redundant, was installed. However the brickwork base of the original structure was used to build a facsimile box in a nearby garden. Although Talerddig station had closed in 1965 a passing loop was retained on this single line between Newtown and Machynlleth. JGS003729

Top right. Standard 4-6-0 No. 75024 approaches a deserted Llanbrynmair station on 8th. August 1964 with the 8:20 am Summer Saturdays only service from Paddington to Pwllheli. At this date there were three through services from Paddington to Pwllheli one of which also had through coaches for Aberystwyth. Journey time from the capital to Pwllheli by the 8:20am was 8 hours 25 minutes although one of the other two services managed it in a shade under 8 hours. Llanbrynmair was to close along with many of the other smaller stations on this route on 14th. June the following year. PG3854

Bottom right. The suffix "Road" usually indicated that a station was some distance from the settlement of the same name and this was true of Cemmes Road station which was 1½ miles away from the village. Formerly the junction for the branch to Dinas Mawddy the first station on the branch was much closer to the village of Cemmaes. To avoid confusion with that station it was decided to name the station on the mainline using the anglicised spelling of the village thus it was always known as Cemmes Road not Cemmaes Road. Today the main station building survives in residential use.

Top right. Churchward 4500 Class 2-6-2T No. 4555 arrives at a rather inclement Dovey Junction where there is a goodly crowd, clad in raincoats and hats, some of whom are awaiting its arrival whilst the majority are no doubt bound for stations to Barmouth. The finger post board attached to the column on the platform indicates a service for "Aberdovey, Towyn and Barmouth" that will leave from the platform on the right. The prairie tank which has brought in a service from Aberystwyth will be proceeding up the main line towards Machynlleth. Although this image is undated No. 4555 was a Machynlleth based locomotive during the ten year period 1947-57. REV 594-2

Bottom right. No. 4549 has just arrived at a sunnier Dovey Junction with a service from Barmouth on 9th. September 1959. The sharp curve of the Barmouth line is apparent in the right background where the girder bridge crossing the River Dovey can just be discerned. The railway crossing of the Dovey estuary had originally been proposed using a long timber viaduct, similar to that near Barmouth, but in the event the river was bridged just before it widened out into the tidal estuary. Smoke at the rear of the train indicates that another locomotive has coupled on to the carriages in order to form a return working. The modern signalbox seen on the platform was a Western Region type 37A design fitted with a 65 lever GWR vertical tappet 5-bar frame. This opened on 22nd February 1959 replacing an 1890 built Dutton & Co. type 1 design box located 78 yards further towards Aberystwyth. The new box closed on 21st October 1988 when signalling passed to the control of Machynlleth. SUM 366

Below. Locally based No. 7806 "Cockington Manor" departs from Machynlleth with a down service on 6th. September 1958 passing over the road bridge which carries the A487 one of the most important roads in Wales known officially as the Fishguard to Bangor trunk road. No 7806 was not one of the fortunate nine Manors that have been preserved being scrapped at Cashmore's Great Bridge in 1965. SUM 364

Aberystwyth shed in this 1955 view plays host to Machynlleth based Dukedog No. 9008, Oswestry based Standard No. 75020 and Machynlleth based Collett No. 2271. Of interest to the left is a stationary boiler with an enormous chimney. The shed which dates from rebuilding in 1938 remained open until April 1965 after which it was converted to house the Vale of Rheidol narrow gauge locomotives. NS200149A

Aberystwyth station on 31st. May 1961 witnesses Manor Class No. 7822 *"Foxcote Manor"* backing down on to the coaching stock of the 12.35pm service to the north east extremity of former Cambrian Railways metals at Whitchurch. This service also contained through coaches for Crewe and Shrewsbury. In the far left platform is the 11.55am departure for Carmarthen which, according to the station clock seen in the background, should be in five minutes time. This journey covering 56 ¼ miles would take 2 hours and 26 minutes and involved 21 intermediate station stops, five of which were conditional upon request. No. 7822 is preserved and currently based on the Llangollen Railway. F 5979

Standard Class 2 2-6-0 No. 78005 is seen at Aberystwyth on 29th. June 1962. A total of 65 of these locomotives were produced of which four survived into preservation although one of these, No. 78059, has been the basis of a conversion to the tank version as No. 84030, none of which were preserved. No. 78005, allocated to Oswestry depot from new in 1953, would shortly be transferred away from Cambrian lines to Gloucester in November 1962. WS6200

DOVEY JUNCTION – PWLLHELI

Dukedog No. 9017 waits at the head of a Pwllheli service at Dovey Junction's curving platform, which could hold a maximum of five coaches, on 9th. August 1960 whilst the photographer's young son (?) makes sure he gets into the picture. This was the final year of Dukedog operation and No. 9017, which is also receiving some admiring glances from passengers and staff, was fortunate enough to have been saved for preservation. NS 200586

Coincidentally all the twos and all the fives numerically are in close juxtaposition in this view of Collett 2251 Class No. 2222 together with 45XX Class No. 5555 seen here at the south end of Towyn station. No 5555 was a recent transferee from Swindon to Machynlleth depot in June 1961 but only stayed there a month before transfer to Shrewsbury thus dating this image to either June or July 1961. No. 2222 here coupled to one of the smaller capacity narrow tenders is looking particularly smart in its lined green livery. It was a Machynlleth based locomotive at this time until it too was transferred, this time to Worcester depot, in June the following year. NS209994

No. 4555 is about to enter the famous Friog avalanche shelter with a down service on 28th. July 1951. With the windows open in the first coach several of the passengers are taking in the spectacular views. The parallel road above the line can also be seen clinging to the cliffside. RCR3299

This vertiginous view, taken on 28th. July 1951 from the road running above the railway, shows the sloping nature of the roof of the Friog avalanche shelter. A northbound service has just exited the shelter en route to Barmouth hauled by an unidentified Dukedog. This viewpoint shows how the railway here was cut into a ledge along the cliff face giving passengers a spectacular view. The alternative of tunnelling through the cliffs was considered but was judged to be too expensive at the time of the line's construction. RCR3295

This close-up of the Friog avalanche shelter also dates from July 1951. It was constructed by the GWR in the 1930s after landslips had twice sent locomotives hurtling down the cliff to the rocky seashore below. Made from reinforced concrete the shelter is 56 metres long and has a sloping top to deflect falling debris from above. The first of the two fatal accidents occurred on January 1st. 1883 when a passenger train from Machynlleth ran into debris which included stone from a collapsed retaining wall which ran beside the road that ran above the line. The locomotive's driver and fireman were both killed as were the crew of a mail and passenger train which ran into debris on 6th. March 1933 causing their locomotive to mount the parapet alongside the track and plunge into the sea. RCR3300

As the signalman walks back to his box over the boarded crossing, having exchanged tokens with the crew of No. 3202 coupled behind No. 4584, the train makes ready to depart from Barmouth Junction with a service to Pwllheli on 28th. July 1951. The lines leading off to the left led to Dolgelley and up the Dee valley to the mainline junction of Ruabon. This was a triangular junction although through running from Dovey Junction to Dolgelley was not possible after closure of the south signalbox by Cambrian Railways prior to 1914. However, the curve was retained as a siding and used for locomotive turning purposes until the early 1960s this being particularly useful after the removal of the turntable at Barmouth during the 1950s. Apart from a train in the up platform the plume of smoke in the right background indicates the presence of another train on what must have been a busy summer's day. RCR3287

Formerly known as Barmouth Junction by the date of this view, 30th. May 1961, the station with its massive running in board had morphed, or should that be "morfed", into Morfa Mawddach. This change of name in June 1960 came about due to concerns that passengers for nearby Barmouth might be tempted to alight prematurely. Following closure of the Dee Valley route, from 18th. January 1965, it was no longer a junction and saw no further services for Dollgellau, Bala, Corwen, Llangollen, Ruabon or Chester. Floods had already closed part of the line between Bala Junction and Llangollen the previous month. Today a single platform halt with a small shelter is all that remains of this once important interchange station. H2312

The footplate crew of this pair of Collett 0-6-0s, with No. 2219 leading, look back along their lengthy train awaiting the right away from Barmouth Junction on an unrecorded date in the 1950s. A temporary speed restriction sign can be seen trackside by the tender of the leading locomotive and in the background lie the foothills of Cader Idris which rises to 893m being the highest peak in southern Snowdonia. In October 1959 No. 2219 would be reallocated from Oswestry shed to the other end of the principality at Ebbw Junction never to return to the spectacular scenery of this neck of the woods. REV 268-3

Sending the seagulls scattering an unidentified Dukedog double heading with a 2-6-2T have just exited Barmouth tunnel which, at 70 yards in length, was one of five such tunnels constructed along the coastal route from Dovey Junction to Pwllheli. The viaduct to the left which had six spans and known as Old Chapel Viaduct was originally a timber construction but was rebuilt in concrete in 1952. REV 77C -5-2

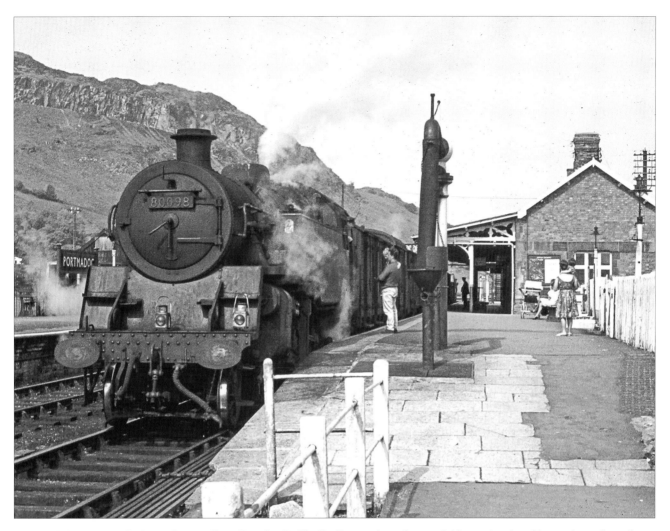

Above. It had been the intention to dieselise the Pwllheli - Dovey Junction and Aberystwyth – Shrewsbury lines from November 1964 but this was delayed until the New Year to coincide with the deferred January 1965 closure of the Whitchurch – Buttington Junction section. Crew training on six car DMU sets was undertaken on the Shrewsbury – Aberystwyth line during January 1965 with diesel working commencing on the 18th. of that month. Steam was retained for goods working for a little longer with the main scheduled passenger working rostered for steam being the *"Cambrian Coast Express"* the final steam working of which did not take place until 4th. March 1967. Steam working continued between Dovey Junction and Pwllheli but DMU sets released from the Walsall area began arriving and gradually took over former steam workings. Steam from Shrewsbury to the coast did continue to operate sporadically mainly using 6D's stock of Standard Class 4s and several were to be seen in action over the 1965 August bank holiday and on specials. This view of Standard 4MT No. 80098 on an up train at Portmadoc dating from 10th June 1965 may possibly indicate a diesel failure or unit shortage. No. 80098 had only one month to go before withdrawal from Machynlleth shed. With the closure of Pwllheli shed three months later on 5th. September 1965 the through coaches of the CCE which formerly served the Dovey Junction – Pwllheli section were withdrawn and replaced by a DMU connection from the junction. TY002645

Top left. Collett 2251 Class No. 3200 departs Barmouth on an unrecorded date in 1953 passing on the left what might be described as the local "bus station" which was in reality just a series of bus stands on some rough ground where a number of bus stops indicating a variety of destinations including Dolgelley were situated. A single decker bus can be seen on the far right waiting to pull up on one of these stands but for the moment held up at the level crossing gates. NS201019

Bottom left. A contrast in locomotive designs seen here at Barmouth with Nos. 78000 and 7827 "Lydham Manor". The Standard 2-6-0 has charge of an up freight service and is seen passing the impressive Victorian chapel which lay to the south of the level crossing. The chapel now does duty as the Dragon Centre a community centre and 186 seat theatre. No. 7827 is parked at the separate platform often used by the Dolgelley shuttle but which today is the site of the Jubilee car park. REV 77C 4-5

Rounding the curve into Criccieth station on an unrecorded date in 1960 comes Standard Class 2 2-6-0 No.78007 with an up service. On the right can be seen the rather unusual station entrance awning in a style reminiscent of cinemas of old. The Standard, whose similarity to the Ivatt LMS design is very apparent, was half way through its 14 year life at this date and would finish up at Bolton from where it was withdrawn in May 1967. NS 207609

The junction station of Afon Wen plays host to Collett 0-6-0 No. 3200 seen here on a down service to Pwllheli on 30th. August 1961. The station would lose its junction status with the closure of the line to Caernarvon in December 1964. The Collett was reallocated from Machynlleth to Oswestry in July 1963 and thence to Templecombe on the S&D from where it would be withdrawn in January 1965 ending its days shuttling along the Highbridge branch. SUM 648

Photographed in a similar position to the previous image Dukedog No. 9014 halts at Afon Wen with a service for Pwllheli on an unrecorded date. The name *"Earl Waldegrave"* was allocated to this locomotove but never carried the name being given to Castle Class No. 5057. This 4-4-0 would remain in service until October 1960. NS 201124

This view of Penychain taken in August 1962 shows the lengthy platforms provided for the influx of trainloads of holidaymakers bound for the nearby Butlins camp. Penychain had opened as a halt in 1933 and led a quiet life until the camp, which was originally constructed by Butlin's in 1940 at the request of the Admiralty to serve as HMS Glendower an RN training base. In 1947 the camp was converted for use by holidaymakers and the halt was upgraded to the status of a station with staff in attendance during the summer months. The tracks through the station were signalled for bi-directional running with the route doubled as far as the junction at Afon Wen where the Caernarvon and Bangor line diverged from the coast line. These days, much reduced in size, Penychain has reverted to unstaffed halt status and serves the former Butlin's site now owned by Bourne Leisure and marketed under the name Hafyn-y-mor Holiday Park. JLS

On 10th. June 1965 Standard 4-6-0 No. 75002 makes ready to leave from Pwllheli's platform No. 2 with a service for Barmouth and Machynlleth.

MID WALES LINE MOAT LANE JUNCTION - BRECON

Collett 0-6-0 No. 2204 arrives at Moat lane Junction with a down service on 11th. June 1960. The Mid Wales line is on the right and, being the first line to serve the locality, has a straight run through the station whereas the line from Machynlleth enters on a sharp curve. There appear to be some chunky looking lumps of coal in the tender of the locomotive waiting at the up platform that will no doubt require some breaking up by the fireman before being offered into the firebox. JB000070

Another sizeable running in board was required at Moat Lane Junction to list the relevant destinations that one could reach by changing trains here. These were Llanidloes, Builth Wells, Rhyader, Brecon and South Wales, the latter necessitating a change of trains at Talyllyn Junction, for stations to Newport, or Brecon for Neath but this latter option was really impracticable there being a very limited once daily service on Mondays – Fridays rising to twice on Saturdays to Neath. Passengers in a hurry to reach South Wales might well be disappointed as the journey from Moat Lane to Newport in 1958 for example, for which there was only really one feasible service, would occupy some five hours. JH 2475

The magnificent station building at Llanidloes is shown to advantage in this view taken from the footbridge. At one time planned as the headquarters of Cambrian Railways it suffered a decline in fortunes when it was decided to make the HQ in an equally grandiose building at Oswestry in 1866. Today the main A470 road thunders past this spot on the former trackbed but the building, now Grade II listed and restored in 1984, thankfully remains in situ acting as a small business centre. LRF 6084

A van, carrying the chalked destination Cardiff, has just been attached to the rear of a Brecon service whilst passengers say their goodbyes to people on the platform and the station master, in discussion with the guard, waits for the starter signal to drop. Llanidloes, like Builth Wells, benefitted from the running of short services to and from the nearby junction, in this case Moat Lane, some five times daily on weekdays, although one journey did not operate on Saturdays or school holidays. Following the withdrawal of passenger services in 1962 Llanidloes continued to see cement trains from Aberthaw in South Wales until 1967 run in connection with the construction of a dam three miles distant. JH 2472

This small two road sub shed to Oswestry, situated at the north eastern end of the Llanidloes station site seen in the previous image, housed Dean Goods No. 2484 on 11th. May 1952. This 0-6-0 would be withdrawn from service exactly two years later in May 1954. The shed, built of brick with a slate roof, dated back to 1859 the opening date of this original isolated section of line between Llanidloes and Newtown which two years later was connected to Oswestry and ultimately absorbed into the Cambrian Railways system. NS201098A

Lonely Tylwch Halt, reduced to a single platform following removal of the passing loop, and set in the valley of the Afon Dulas, which here forms the border between Merionethshire and Montgomeryshire or these days Gwynedd and Powys, sees the arrival of Ivatt 2MT No. 46520 with a working to Moat Lane Junction. It would be most unlikely to drop off or pick up any passengers in this remote spot which had the luxury of four trains each way daily although one of the southbound trains only stopped on request. The rails in the foreground are the run off to house a platelayers' trolley. Tylwch was the scene of an accident on 16th. September 1899 when a mail train which had recently arrived at the station was struck head-on by an excursion train which had earlier left Builth Wells heading for Manchester. A local woman from Pantydwr who had joined the excursion train at the previous station was killed and five other passengers were seriously injured. JH 2469

On 14th. October 1962 just weeks away from the line's closure at the end of the year two Ivatt 2MTs Nos. 46507 and 46514 cross at Pantydwr which was situated at the highest point of the Mid Wales line at 974 feet above sea level. Timetabled trains were scheduled to cross at Pantydwr just once daily between 3:23 pm and 3:28 pm. The line descended for some seven miles to the next station at Rhyader. KEN NUTTALL

The running in board states "Rhyader for the Elan Valley Lakes" these aquatic features being a chain of five man-made reservoirs created by damming the Elan and Claerwen rivers within the Elan Valley. Constructed by the Birmingham Corporation Water Department they provide clean drinking water for the Birmingham area. The Mid Wales line obviously wished to capitalise on their tourist potential by mentioning their proximity on their station signage. During construction of the dams a standard gauge line was built from Elan Valley Junction to the south of Rhyader station to the dam sites. It was operative from 1896 to about 1912 with the last track being lifted in 1916. In July 1942 the prototype charge of the famous Barnes Wallis "bouncing bomb" was tested at a small dam in the Elan Valley where 280lbs of high explosive destroyed the

central portion of the Nant-y-Gro masonry dam, built to provide water to the workmen's village, with the remains of the dam being still visible today. The main station building at Rhyader was retained after closure as a non rail connected coal depot until April 1965 and is today occupied by Powys County Highways Department. JH 2468

Newbridge-on-Wye station sees a service to Builth Wells call on 2nd. June 1961. At the time of the TUCC hearing into the closure of the Mid Wales route BR claimed that the line was a hopeless case losing some £150,000 p.a. (£4m at today's prices) travelling as it did through a sparsely populated rural area. Add to poor patronage the fact that it was steam worked with all that involved in terms of staffing, there were 40 staff employed at Llanidloes station and shed at the time of closure for example, and it is not hard to see how the case was hard to dispute on purely economic grounds. The fact that other contemporary rail closures left Brecon completely isolated from the network was of course another matter. LRF 6080

As a handful of passengers leave the train No. 46520 halts at Newbridge-on-Wye with the 12.45pm service from Builth Wells to Moat Lane Junction on 2nd. June 1961 crossing with an engineers' train. The station here had staggered platforms whilst the siding on the right served a cattle dock. As the name suggests the valley of the River Wye was followed by the railway here as it would be for some thirty miles between Rhyader and Three Cocks Junction. LRF 6078

CORNERS of the CAMBRIAN

Below. The juxtaposition of the famous hydraulic lift with an Ivatt 2-6-0 immediately gives away the location of this view as Builth Road Low Level where No.46513 has charge of a southbound service on 2nd. June 1961. Whilst able bodied passengers could negotiate the steps and ramp leading to the High Level platforms the lift, constructed in 1897, could take luggage and those who did not, or could not, wish to climb up to the Central Wales line platforms. When the Mid Wales line was constructed it cut through the south western rim of an ancient moated enclosure known as Cwrt Llechryd, a former stronghold of possibly a prince of Powys or a local chieftain dating from the early medieval period, with the station being initially known as Llechryd Junction although it changed to the more familiar Builth Road in 1889. JH 2460

Top right. Today the main building is a public house, appropriately the Cambrian Arms, but back on 2nd. June 1961 when this image was taken it was still Builth Road Low Level station as the running in board indicates. One could change here and transfer to the High Level station above for trains to Shrewsbury and Swansea and those destinations mentioned on the running in board. Although the Low Level platforms closed to passengers in December 1962 the goods yard here remained connected to the High Level line until 6th. September 1965. JH 2464

Bottom right. A service for Brecon waits at the Low Level down platform headed by the usual Ivatt 2-6-0 in this undated view taken from the vantage point of the High Level station. When the station opened only a single platform was provided but a second platform was subsequently added for up trains together with a passing loop. JH 2507

This southward view of the High Level station at Builth Road dates from 9th. May 1961 and shows the sign on the side of the wooden building, directing passengers to the "Way Out and Low Level Station", positioned above the row of fire buckets. The wooden planked section of platform in the foreground lies on the bridge over the Mid Wales line beneath. The up side loop was taken out of use in October 1965 and today just a single line and bus shelter accommodate intending passengers with the main station building having been converted into residential use. A far cry indeed from its former interchange function. JH 2278

Standard Class 5 No. 73091 pauses at the High Level station at Builth Road with a service from Swansea to Shrewsbury. Although this image is undated it probably stems from the period September 1958 – October 1961 when this 4-6-0 was allocated to Shrewsbury shed. Single unit Class 153 DMUs now operate on the Heart of Wales line as it is now marketed with currently five trains provided each way along the whole route daily with two trains each way on Sundays. JH 2506

Builth Wells, one of four spa towns in the area the others being Llandrindod, Llangammarch and Llanwrtyd which had stations on the Central Wales line, was one of the more important stops on the Mid Wales route but having said that the town can still only muster less than 2,500 inhabitants at the recent (2021) census. Here No. 46520 heads the 12.45pm all stations service to Moat Lane Junction, where it is due to arrive at 2:10pm, on 2nd. June 1961. The trilby hatted staff member climbing the ladder appears to be examining a problem with the water crane. At the other platform the service from Builth Road which has arrived at 12:33pm has an enforced wait of 42 minutes before leaving for Brecon at 1:15pm. LRF 6076

Top left. Oswestry based No. 46518 is seen in the yard at Builth Wells with its two coach train on 29th. May 1961 prior to taking up its next working. In addition to the two trains each way which traversed the whole length of the Mid Wales line Builth Wells benefitted from short workings to and from Builth Road to provide connections with Central Wales line services. In 1958 for examples trains left Builth Wells eight times each weekday at 7:45, 8:55, 9:40, 12:05, 12:45, 2:37, 6:21 and 7:15 for Builth Road with nine services arriving back at Builth Wells at 6:33, 7:10, 9:13, 10:00, 11;22, 12:33, 4:14, 7:02 and 7:35. JH 2275

Bottom left. Services were scheduled to pass here at Erwood between 11:35 am and 11:40 am and on 29th. May 1961 Ivatt 2MT No. 46504 running tender first waits patiently for the arrival of classmate No. 46526 the fireman of which is about to collect the token for the onward journey to Three Cocks. JH 2272

Below. Also taken on 29th. May 1961 is this view of the main station buildings at Erwood. Although pleasantly situated on the banks of the River Wye unfortunately the hamlet of Erwood was a mile distant and situated astride the main A470 road from Builth Wells to Brecon so a trek to the station for residents was probably the least favoured option. JH 2273

Also operating tender first is No. 46504 with the 11.15 am departure from Three Cocks Junction to Builth Road seen at Erwood on 29th. May 1961. Passengers from Brecon wishing to travel through mid Wales would have left on the 10:25 am service to Hereford and changed at Three Cocks. Although a signalbox still stands at Erwood, where the station site was at one stage after closure converted into a cafe and craft centre housed within old coaching stock together a short length of track on which a Fowler 0-4-0 diesel resided, it did in fact came from Newbridge-on-Wye. LRF 5866

Three Cocks was another one of those junctions sited in the middle of nowhere being the point where the Mid Wales line diverged to the left whilst that to Hereford headed straight on. There were plans at one time to construct an east to north curve thus allowing through trains to run from Builth Wells to Hereford but this was never constructed. Named after a 15th C. coaching inn on the adjacent A438 road, the site of the former station now houses a garden centre. JH 361

Ivatt 2-6-0 No. 46512 with the 8:05 am service from Brecon to Builth Wells is signalled away from Three Cocks Junction. After a wait of 25 minutes at Builth Wells the train would then continue to Builth Road where it terminated returning after 12 minutes to Builth Wells thus forming a useful connection to and from a Swansea to Shrewsbury service along the Central Wales line. JH 359

Above. This May 1961 view shows the small waiting shelter at Trefeinon which until November 1959 boasted a crossing loop and signalbox. It was not until April 1960 that some economies were introduced when the station became unstaffed and the small goods yard closed. LRF 5855

Top left. This view of Talgarth dates from 29th. May 1961 and is taken from a service to Moat Lane Junction looking south along the Brecon platform. The water tank served the ornate platform mounted water cranes located here and today the base of the water tank has been subsumed into an extension of the original station buildings which survive as a residence whilst the trackbed is now occupied by the A479 trunk road. LRF 5862

Bottom left. Taken from the window of a Brecon bound service this image affords us a better view of the ornate water column at Talgarth with its "fire devil" brazier. At least some parcels traffic was still being handled to bolster the meagre receipts being derived from the sparse passenger loadings being experienced by 1961 the penultimate year of operation. After closure of the line at the end of 1962 the yard here remained as a BR goods depot served by road until November 1964. JH 2259

The signalman stands ready to exchange tokens with a member of the footplate crew as Ivatt 2-6-0 No. 46521 rolls in to Talyllyn Junction with the 12:30 service from Builth Road Low Level to Brecon on 2nd. May 1959. This train had spent no less than 42 minutes idling at Builth Wells before proceeding to Brecon and had provided a connection at Three Cocks Junction with the 12:42 service from Hereford which terminated there. The curving platform on the left was added in 1895 to accommodate Mid Wales trains to allow a second up train to be accommodated at the junction. The line to Newport curves away to the right. This is where Cambrian metals ended although trains had running powers into Brecon. KJ 1427

No. 46518 emerges from Talyllyn tunnel into the junction station on 2nd. May 1959 with the 13:25 pm service from Brecon to Moat Lane Junction, a destination it would not reach until 4:03 pm taking 2 hours 38 minutes to cover the intervening 60 miles. There was a connection available at Three Cocks Junction for a service to Hereford and although passengers could change at Builth Road Low Level for the High Level station with its services to Swansea and Shrewsbury this would involve very tedious waits of between 1 hour 25 minutes and 2 hours. This illustrated the difficulty of timetabling reasonable connections when services on both routes were so sparse. KJ1425

The impressive Brecon Free Street station originally served no less than four different railway companies – the Brecon & Merthyr, the Neath & Brecon, the Hereford, Hay & Brecon, and the Mid Wales. The station which opened in 1871 had two through platforms with the outer face of that on the south side generally being used by the Neath trains. On the north side was a terminal bay and a small turntable. In common with some other junction stations there were specific times of day when the railway came alive with trains terminating and departing before a sabbatarian calm descended once more. In this view a porter seems to be attending to some animal or bird within the basket cage. Today a very different type of station occupies the site - one used by the local fire brigade. JH2535

Above. Brecon shed seen from a departing train plays host to a number of trucks laden with coal and a couple of Ivatt 2-6-0s, the latter day mainstay of services to Hereford and along the Mid Wales line. Pannier tanks and 2251 Class 0-6-0s, the normal motive power for services to and from Newport and Swansea, were also based here. This two road shed dating from 1893 was classified 89B in the 1950s and in January 1959 had an allocation of two Collett 0-6-0s, one pannier tank and five Ivatt 2-6-0s. It became a sub shed of Cardiff in the 1960s and was renumbered 88K no longer having its own allocation of locomotives. It continued in this servicing role until closure in December 1962 following the withdrawal of all remaining routes to Brecon. JH 2537

Top left. On an unrecorded date No. 46521 is waiting departure time with the 13:20pm to Moat Lane Junction. Two coaches were more than adequate for the handful of passengers likely to be carried by this service. The bay platform is seen on the right. Latterly only two trains daily made the complete journey from Brecon to Moat Lane, other services from Brecon on the Mid Wales route terminating at Builth Road. No. 46521 was based at Brecon shed from March 1953, the month after it entered BR service at Oswestry, until October 1959 when it transferred back to Oswestry. It would be withdrawn in October 1966 from Machynlleth depot. JH 2536

Bottom left. This panorama of the east end of Brecon station reveals No. 46513 occupying the bay platform on 21st. August 1962 the final year of passenger services to this the county town of Brecknockshire. This Ivatt 2-6-0 was an Oswestry based locomotive at this date so will probably be heading up the Mid Wales route in due course. It ended its short career of 13½ years based at Carlisle Upperby shed four years later in July 1966. PG 3019

Above. The former station at Watton dating from 1863 was used by the Brecon & Merthyr Railway but closed in 1871 when services were diverted to the new Free Street station. It continued in use as offices for the nearby loco shed and for goods traffic with the line to the new station running along the embankment where the coaching stock is parked to the rear of the station. At one time there was also a third station in Brecon at Mount Street used by the Neath & Brecon Railway. NS 201088A

Top right. Wrexham Central is seen here on 20th. September 1958 looking west with the great spire of neighbouring St. Marks church, now demolished, dominating the scene. Services from Ellesmere arrived from the east and terminated here whilst services from Chester Northgate and New Brighton arrived from the west and also terminated here. There were five platform faces but only two through platforms. Central always had a rather temporary feel about it and at one time there were plans to erect a more substantial station but this was never done and by 1969 just a single platform survived before the track was cut back and a new station opened in 1998 further to the west. A shopping centre and car park were built on the site of the original station. AEB 4223

Bottom right. A recent arrival from the west is Standard tank No. 84004 which helps to date this view probably to 1954/5 at which time this 2-6-2T was based at Wrexham's Rhosddu shed judging by the shedcode 6E on the smokebox door. It would end its days at Wrexham's other shed at Croes Newydd in October 1965 after just 12 years in service. The presence of poster boards on the right being somewhat improbably headed LNER can be explained by the fact that Rhosddu depot, although originally opened by the Wrexham, Mold & Connah's Quay Railway, subsequently became a Great Central shed on the acquisition of the former company by the latter. In 1923 the GCR was absorbed into the London & North Eastern Railway which resulted in the curious paradox of a Welsh depot belonging to the LNER. NS 207848

BRANCH LINES : WREXHAM

Looking east at Wrexham Central, this time with another church prominent being that of St. Giles the parish church of Wrexham which is still standing, a train for the west stands at platform headed by C13 Class No. 67435. This class of 40 4-4-2Ts was to a Robinson design for the Great Central Railway and based locally at Rhosddu shed No. 67435 would be withdrawn at the end of 1952 although the last survivor did just make it into 1960. NS 205689

Situated just ¾ mile from Central station Hightown in the area of Wrexham known as Caia Park sees the arrival of a push-pull service propelled by the usual Collet 0-4-4T. This small halt opened in July 1923 and lasted until withdrawal of services on the branch in September 1962. The halt was conveniently situated for workers between sidings at Caia Road and the Abenbury brickworks with Rubery Owen & Co. also having a large facility in the vicinity. MC 20020

Collett 14XX Class No. 1432 is signalled away from a rather decrepit Bangor-on-Dee station towards the end of the branch's existence. No. 1432 was a frequent performer on this line being based at Oswestry for many years until withdrawal came in July 1963. One coach invariably sufficed for the limited traffic by then offering. MC 20609

As is readily apparent from this view Bangor-on-Dee was provided with a passing facility and in common with all other stations and halts saw some eight departures daily in each direction. Judging by the passengers crossing or just about to cross the boarded crossing at the far end of the platforms a train has recently left and indeed this view was probably taken from the rear coach of that departure. AEB 4224

This exterior view of Llanfyllin station dates from 30th. May 1961. The branch, promoted to access the extensive limestone deposits of the area, was surveyed and engineered by one Thomas Savin, who became a contractor for many of the lines absorbed into the Cambrian empire and who also built the grand Cambrian Hotel at Borth near Aberystwyth which was the destination of an excursion train from Llanfyllin on 17th. July 1863 the official opening day of the branch. Some 600 passengers left Llanfyllin and the intermediate stations conveyed in no less than 23 coaches. Station Road in Llanfyllin now leads to an industrial estate. H2329

4579 No. 46516 waits at Llanfyllin terminus with a return working to Oswestry on an unrecorded date. On this single line branch train working was by electric train token between the junction at Llanymynech and Llansantffraid and by electric train tablet between there and Llanfyllin. The crossing station was at Llansantffraid. HORNE

Above. Before the era of branch operation by Ivatt 2-6-0s ex GWR 5800 Class 0-4-2Ts were often to be seen here and at Llanfyllin terminus on 21st. July 1951 is No. 5812 which has recently arrived from Oswestry. Before nationalisation this locomotive had been a frequent performer on the Tiverton branches in Devon but from 1948 its home base became Oswestry. In 1953 it was consigned to store at Swindon from where it was officially withdrawn in 1957 having completed a mileage of 506,000 during its working life of close on 24 years. RCR3220

Top right. The intermediate station at Llanfechain is seen here from the train on 30th. May 1961. In the last full year of services, 1964, trains left here for the mainline at 7:54am, 9:55am, 1:40pm, 4:15pm (SX), 4:40pm (SO) and 8:25pm (SO). After closure the station became an attractive private residence with the trackbed infilled to platform level. JH 2334

Bottom right. 4580 Having just passed the site of Nantmawr Junction this is the view from a train approaching Carreghofa Halt seen in the distance. The overbridge was in two sections the stone construction on the far side carrying the road whilst the metal section on the near side supported the Montgomery Canal. The halt, opened in April 1938 in an attempt to attract more local traffic, remained open until closure of the line but today no trace remains. HORNE

Above. An unidentified Ivatt 2MT rounds the curve from the Llanfyllin branch to enter Llanymynech where passengers could change for stations to Welshpool and the Cambrian coast. The branch train will continue on to Oswestry calling at the intermediate stations of Pant (Salop) and Llynclys. The platforms formerly served by trains of the Shropshire & Montgomeryshire Railway can be seen immediately to the left of the signalbox. Whilst the village of Llanymynech lay in Wales the station was in fact just over the border in Shropshire. HORNE 4582

Top right. The Tanat Valley Railway yard at the Llangynog terminus was still quite busy to judge from the amount of wagons seen in this image which dates from August 1951. The company was always in debt and in 1921 was obliged to sell the line to the Cambrian Railways who had previously assisted in the construction of the 15 mile route. The railway closed to passengers in January 1951 so wagons could be accommodated at the platform as seen here without causing hindrance to any other traffic. TG 146-1

Bottom right. The intermediate station of Llanrhaidr ym Mochnant, the running in board of which is reflected in the carriage windows, sees the arrival of a service for Llangynog headed by an unidentified 0-6-0T but which in all probability is No. 819. This view, although undated, would appear to have been taken in pre-nationalisation days judging by the GWR insignia on the four compartment coach. A passing loop was provided here and following the withdrawal of the passenger service in 1951, caused mainly by the coal crisis of that year, the line west of here was closed to freight from July the following year with complete closure of the route coming in 1960. As was often the case at closed stations the yard here continued to be used for coal storage, now delivered by road, well into the late 1960s.

LLANGYNOG

The eastern end of Llanrhaidr ym Mochnant station gives a good view of the ground frame levers and signalling. Just visible beyond the further signal post is a level crossing with the station approach road coming in from the far left where there was a goods siding and cattle dock. The village is situated a mile to the north west of the station and now goes by the alternative spelling of Llanrhaeadr ym Mochnant. The Tanat Valley Light Railway preservation society has acquired two miles of trackbed and has long term hopes of reopening the line as far as here for heritage and tourist use although it is currently focused on the Blodwell Junction to Nantmawr section.

Blodwell Junction station and the Nantmawr branch are shown on the Railway Clearing House map dating from 1915. It was the opening of the TVLR in 1904 which created the junctions at Blodwell. The single platform station seen above continued to handle goods traffic until this service was withdrawn in January 1964. Quarry traffic from Nantmawr continued until October 1971 although Blodwell continued to see railway wagons from nearby Llanddu quarry which were shunted here until a new loop was installed in 1985 between the quarry and the Blodwell goods siding site which saw the end of railway activity at Blodwell Junction station. Traffic from Llanddu quarry ceased in 1989.

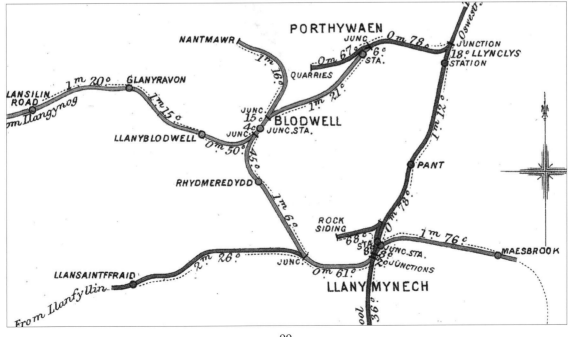

DINAS MAWDDY

Above. As no views of the branch could be located within the archive this is the closest we can get with Manning Wardle 0-6-0ST in its guise as GWR No. 824 seen at Oswestry on 14th. September 1937. Delivered to contractor R. S. Francis in 1865 for use in the construction of the Potteries, Shrewsbury & North Wales Railway, known informally as the "Potts", it was subsequently sold to the Mawddwy Railway and acquired the name "Mawddy". Rebuilt in both 1893 and 1911 it was then transferred to the Van Railway before being absorbed into Cambrian Railways stock where it was allocated the No. 30. It was scrapped in 1940. NS 209978

Left. This view is of Sharp Stewart 2-4-0, formerly Cambrian Railways No. 58 now GWR No. 1196, seen at Oswestry on 11th. September 1938 having arrived with a service from the Tanat Valley. Built in May 1896 it was withdrawn from Oswestry shed in April 1948.

Above. A Kerry branch freight headed by an unidentified pannier tank rounds the curve leading to the junction at Abermule. Freight traffic consisted mainly of timber, bricks, cattle and sheep and several of the wagons, many with pre nationalisation markings from all four companies, are carrying quantities of timber. There was apparently sufficient freight traffic to justify keeping this 3¾ mile branch active until 1st. May 1956 when final closure came some quarter century after the passenger service had been withdrawn. GW 344

Top right. This view of the running in board at Dolgelly station was taken on 1st. September 1958 some two years before the anglicised spelling of the town's name was amended to the Welsh spelling of Dolgellau. The attractive river side position of the station is apparent with the tranquil waters of the River Wnion flowing past. SUM336

Bottom right. One of the useful Churchward 4300 Class 2-6-0s No.6316 calls at Dolgelley with a service for Ruabon in this undated view, possibly taken in the late 1950s or early in 1960 judging by the spelling of the running in board and totems during the period when the locomotive was allocated to Croes Newydd shed. After 41 years operational life it would be withdrawn from Llanelli shed in July 1962. NS 201204

DOLGELLEY

All change at Dolgellau now spelt the Welsh way in this view taken on 29th. May 1961 looking towards Ruabon. In addition to through trains from the coast to Ruabon along the Dee Valley there was also a shuttle service to Barmouth which ran four times daily in 1964. H2290

This post closure view taken from a similar viewpoint to a previous image shows how quickly vegetation could spring up once trains had been withdrawn. The station was demolished in the 1970s and the site is now occupied by the Dolgellau by pass. TY002281

Judging by the vegetation growing on the tracks this is also a post closure view this time of the single wooden platform and shelter that constituted Arthog station. These days the former trackbed is now part of Llwybr Mawddach or the Mawddach Trail but of the former station there is no trace. NF 268/27

As can be seen from this high level view Penmaenpool station was wedged in between the river and the main road with just enough space provided for a small goods yard. A service up the Dee Valley route to Ruabon double headed by Nos. 6394 and 75020 enters the station on 18th. August 1962. The platforms here were staggered and a board, with the traditional pointing hand, can just be made out to the right of the chimney stack directing passengers to the short down platform for Barmouth and Pwllheli trains visible behind the goods shed. JLS

Above. The famous signalbox at Penmaenpool, seen after closure of the route in 1965, remains in situ today and is used by the RSPB as an information centre and observation post. Species of birds that can be seen in the estuary include warblers, snipe, geese, curlew and water rail together with mammals such as otters. This box had previously been part of the GWR's exhibit at the Wembley British Empire Exhibition of 1924/5 after which it was stored for a decade at Reading signal works before it was decided to re-erect it at Penmaenpool. TY000326

Bottom left. Just to the west of Penmaenpool station a small two road locomotive shed was provided mainly for use by locomotives operating the Dollgelley – Barmouth service. In this view No. 6303 with an 84J shedplate, Penmaenpool being one of the sub sheds of Croes Newydd along with Bala and Trawsfynydd, keeps company with Collett 0-4-2T No. 5801. The shed seen here was built by Cambrian Railways and opened in June 1869. Originally of timber construction with a gable style pitched slate roof it was later refurbished by the GWR in the 1920s in their usual style of (aesthetically pleasing?) corrugated iron cladding. It was demolished soon after closure of the line. D99-5

NARROW GAUGE
WELSHPOOL & LLANFAIR LIGHT RAILWAY (WLLR)

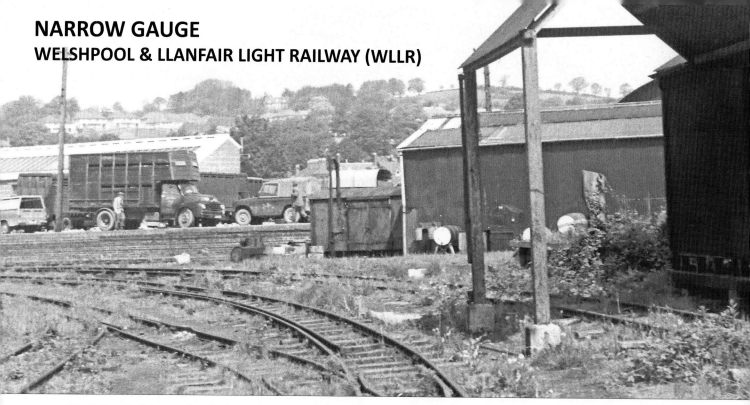

Cambrian Railways inherited two narrow gauge systems and this view shows the connection that the W&LLR, absorbed by the Cambrian in 1923, had with the mainline at Welshpool. The building on the right was part of the transhipment shed for the transfer of goods between the two systems. This view is undated but judging by the grass grown nature of the track, built to the somewhat unusual gauge of 2' 6", it was taken after closure to freight in November 1956, the passenger service having gone as early as 1931, but before the line was cut back to Raven Square in 1964, the Welshpool base of the present day preserved line. HORNE 4564

This view graphically illustrates why the local council were none too keen to allow the preservationists to continue to run trains through the streets of Welshpool. In this area known as the "Narrows" the track was laid on longitudinal beams on the inside of which were protective steel plates carrying the line across the stream between Church Street and Brook Street. HORNE 4562

Vegetation encroaches on the track in the vicinity of the crossing of Church Street. The buildings opposite still occupy the same site today although the gate across the tracks has long gone. HORNE 4563

The other narrow gauge line operated by the Cambrian was the Vale of Rheidol control of which it assumed in 1912. Nos 7, 8 and 9 are seen on the VoR shed at Aberystwyth on 29th. June 1956 shortly after having received their nameplates. With the closure of the standard gauge locomotive shed in April 1965 the trio were able to move into its more spacious premises in 1968 following conversion to narrow gauge requirements. AEB B1410

VALE OF RHEIDOL (VoR)

The withdrawal of the service from Aberystwyth to Carmarthen in February 1965, in actuality December 1964 for the section from Aberystwyth to Strata Florida was prematurely closed by flooding from that month, allowed the VoR to occupy the platform formerly used by the standard gauge trains from 1968. Here *"Prince of Wales"*, which was originally numbered 3212 by the GWR although changed to No. 9 in 1949 and wearing the BR double arrow symbol as the line was the only BR steam operation after August 1968, makes ready to leave with a service for Devil's Bridge. The line was privatised in 1989. NS201230

No. 8, unnamed at the time, is seen at the terminus of Devil's Bridge situated at nearly 700 feet above Aberystwyth in this view dating from 27th. July 1951. This 2-6-2T was designed by Collett and constructed by the GWR along with its two counterparts in 1923/4 as the original VoR rolling stock of two Davies and Metcalfe and one Bagnall locomotive were considered to be in a poor state of repair. It would not be until five years later in June 1956 that the trio received the names that they still carry today. RCR3286

MOTIVE POWER VETERANS

Shed staff and footplate crew stand proudly by their locomotive GWR No. 3212 seen here at Machynlleth shed the first of three images taken on 5th. June 1946. Of particular interest is the amazingly lengthy shovel seen propped up against the cab and the makeshift sheeting strung up in what was often a vain attempt to isolate the cab from the worst of the weather. Hats and caps are the order of the day as regards headwear and jackets, shirts and ties are also much in evidence. Formerly named "Earl of Eldon" Dukedog Class No 3212 dating from 1937 was an amalgamation of the frames of 3405 and the boiler of 3261. Collett decided that these locomotives should be given the names of various GWR directors who had been clamouring for some recognition by having locomotives named after them. However when the directors assembled at Paddington for the unveiling of this supposedly "new" class they were less than impressed at being associated with a very old fashioned looking locomotive. Following the naming of No. 3212 in May 1937 the nameplates were removed and the names allocated to various members of the far more prestigious Castle class. No. 3212 would be numbered 9012 in August 1946 shortly after this view was taken. RCR1253

One of William Dean's Class 2021 tanks introduced from 1897-1905 stands by the sheer rock face, which marks this image out as having been taken at Machynlleth depot. Originally built as saddle tanks they were later converted to pannier tanks. No 2151 seen here was built at the GWR's Wolverhampton Works in 1904, part of the final lot to be constructed, and would last in service until withdrawn in May 1952. 140 examples were eventually delivered with the final one being retired from service in 1959. RCR1254

CORNERS of the CAMBRIAN

Top. Our final image taken at Machynlleth on 5th. June 1946 shows Dean Goods No. 2464 and Dukedog No. 3205. The 0-6-0 would last only another 3½ years being withdrawn at the end of 1949 whilst the 4-4-0 would soldier on until the end came in July 1959 after a change in number to 9005 in August 1946. RCR1249

Middle. Five years later, on 25th. July 1951, the same rock face at Machynlleth depot plays host to this example of the Dean Goods 0-6-0 design No. 2323 part of the class of 160 locomotives designated Class 2301. Dating from 1884 this example continued in service until June 1953 when it was withdrawn from Oswestry depot. RCR3273

Bottom. The very last Dean goods to remain in service, No. 2538, is seen at Oswestry on 30th. June 1956. This 2301 Class of 260 0-6-0 tender locomotives was constructed at Swindon Works between 1883 and 1899 and differed from previous GWR practice in having inside rather than outside frames. Although the initial 20 of the class had no dome they all acquired domed boilers in due course. The final quartet to remain operational comprised Nos. 2474, 2513, 2516 and 2538 with this latter example being withdrawn from Oswestry shed in May 1957. B1431 (2)